Earth Woman

Bury me in your bottomless eyes,
Bare me down the bone column
Dome chamber of your soul,
Press my mouth to hollow earth
And sing for me a lullaby.
Bury me in the swallow of your eyes,
Hold me burning inside you,
Ashes to ashes inside you.

Vows

I bare my chest to you.
I let the scratches heal.
I tend the fire.
I will be here tomorrow.

Dreams of Fools

I love you,
Mother of my children
Keeper of my pride
My only place to hide,
I love you ...   like the dreams of fools.

The Little Girl's Room

In the corner
By the window
Stands a white iron convent bed,
The old-fashion kind
With mosquito bars
And wooden wheels
And a hand-stitched country quilt
Under which a little girl
Lies curled in cotton sleep.

Soon she will open her eyes.
She will stretch awkward arms
And turn to the window.
The sun will rise
And this little girl,
My little girl,
Will look through her window
With open eyes.

Mother Father and Infant Son

I love you, my son,
But I do not love you
The way she does.
She of the body that opened for your birth,
The one that makes sweet milk for you,
The arms that ring a universe of things
When she lifts you from your crib.
I love you my son,
I love you a lot,
But I do not love you the way she does.

To Sea Again

A WALK ON THE BEACH WITH A THREE-YEAR-OLD SON

I have come to the seashore once again
To walk the margin of the morning tide
With John David at my side,
And I discover waves again,
Each crystal surprise
A chill that rises to my ankles
And steals sand from beneath my toes
As it goes laughing back into the sea,
And there are shells ...
And sea cucumbers ...
And little footprints that pattern circles
In the sand around me ...
And my ears can hear the sound of surf again,
And my eyes again perceive the color of rising sky,
And the salt air is my mother's breath
On the face of her waking child,
And the world is wild again
And new,
As I walk the beach with you, my son,
As I walk the beach with you.

Star Song

The children crawl into their sleeping bags,
Their mother lies beside me,
The lantern hisses fading light
On the walls of our tent,
And my breath fogs
Into cold night air,
As I listen to the voice of the universe
And wonder ...
Is it really there?

The Conqueror

He hiked ahead of me
On the side of the mountain.
"I'm gonna make it, Daddy.
 I'm going all the way to the top,"
He said, as little legs kicked rocks,
Hopped over cactus bushes,
Climbed for all their worth
And finally made it to the very top.
Soon the sun set
And I started down
Led by the light of a moon almost full,
With Mother Earth's conquistador asleep in my arms,
Exhausted from his victory,
Vanquished by her pull.

Daddy's Sleeping Beauty

She told me about her first kiss,
The way he tilted his head
To make the noses fit,
And she smiled with a smile
I had not seen before.
I thought of an earlier smile
On the face of a little girl
When Cinderella's slipper fit ...
When Beauty turned her Beast into a prince ...
When Rapunzel let down her golden hair ...
She hugged me and ran off to bed,
Off to her dreams,
The dreams that might someday take her away.
As she closed the door I knew that it was so.
What love it is that loves by letting go.

Red Strawberries

Today we walked the beach with friends.
We watched the great ball of sun
Settle to a point of sparkle
On a blue horizon,
We ate cold strawberries by the light of stars,
Talked Hamlet,
Traded remedies for warts,
And washed dishes.

You went ahead to bed
And when I joined you
My skin — cold from night air —
Roasted beside the oven of your body.

When I am no longer here
Remember this:

> *I walked the beach with friends,*
> *Watched sunsets,*
> *Ate strawberries by starlight,*
> *And melted into dreamless sleep*
> *Wound in the long warm legs*
> *Of lifelong love.*

The Voice of Tahiti

This morning I crawled out of bed,
Stubbed my toe on GI Joe's tank,
Retrieved my hair brush from the bathroom
Of my teenage daughter,
And signed tuition checks.
Oh Gauguin!
You irresponsible bastard!
I wish I had never heard your name.

Lunch Time At the Alamo Cafe'

They have come again today,
Long legs
And bulges
And smells
Like bottom land fresh plowed in spring.
It's the Alamo Cafe' —

Beauty to the left of me,
Nasty to the right,
Warm and understanding
On the stool across the way.

Oh Great Spirit,
Moon father
And mother of the sun,
I know it looks like fun,
But help me make it through the day,
One more time …
Help me make it through the day.

Convention

Her real-estate convention is in Las Vegas
And she doesn't think I should go.
"Somebody has to stay with the children,"
She said
And I laughed
And we teased
And we talked about something else,
But the feeling remains
And I cannot make it go away.
It's not that I don't trust her …
It's just that once upon a time
It was not this way,
And now …
There's this convention in Las Vegas
And she wants to go alone.

When we were boys
They told us what to do —
    Strap on your shoulder pads,
    Charge out on the field,
    Never cry when it hurts,
    And always offer your seat to a lady on the bus.
Everybody said so.
It was just what we were supposed to do.

What I need is a 427 Ford Shelby Cobra —
Zero to sixty in 4.2 seconds,
Fire engine red,
With a wide white stripe
Black leather interior
And a long-legged redhead in the passenger seat.

> *There's fog on the river,*
> *A muddy December morning fog*
> *Like somebody cast a spell.*
> *This old ferry rings its bell*
> *And blows its muffled horn.*
> *I stand with my hand on the starboard rail,*
> *I feel vibrations from the engine*
> *As it strains against the current,*
> *And I wonder how far it is to the other side ...*
> *And how often they paint over chips on the rail ...*
> *And why they should paint it at all ...*
> *And I wonder what dreams there are*
> *In the dark deep swirl of swollen river.*

I will live to celebrate my ninety-sixth birthday.
I will talk with old friends,
I will walk with my grandchildren,
And I will love their grandmother till the day I die,
But ...
How can I say it?
It's a little like how Christmas is never the same
Once you know ...
It's just not the same.

So she will go
And I'll stay with the kids,
And it's OK,
And it's fair,
And I feel silly,
But it's strange …

I am what I was supposed to be,
But everything else changed,
And now I just wish
They hadn't told me to charge out on the field,
And I wish they hadn't told me
To offer my seat to ladies on the bus,
And I especially wish they hadn't told me
Never to cry when it hurts.

Twenty Year Reunion

They are women now
These girls of another lifetime,
Seven thousand days have come and gone …
Yet as I watch their dresses twirl to the old songs
And listen to their laughter
I see girls again —
    Like tribal carpets
    Woven from the starlight of eternal desert night,
    Each knot tied with exquisite care,
    Beautiful when new,
    And more beautiful for every year of wear.
Oh these girls of another lifetime.
They are women now …

Thunder on Monday Morning

We were young
And the boardwalk was long
And the moon
On the water of a shallow bay
Was a silver path
That widened to encompass the universe in its glow,
And there —
In the breath of night,
Above the sound of water round the ankles of wood pilings,
Beneath the small brilliance of a billion silent immolations —
I was deafened by the thunder that pounded in my chest,
Soul-swallowed with the sweet taste of salt on skin,
Paralyzed by the power of her touch.

I open my eyes very slowly.
It is Monday morning.
I am no longer young,
I have collected things,
I have run and won,
I have paid bills
Reared children
Been responsible as the sun,
And I have counted heart beats in days and decades
To the very edge of now ...
Yet I am no longer certain of the color of the sky ...
And I no longer trust the hand that writes these words.

From downstairs in the kitchen
The smell of coffee rises to awake me,
But I curl into a ball instead
To dream again of summer nights,
And the moon,
And the stars,
The taste of salt,
And the sound of thunder,
The hounding pounding unrelenting sound of thunder.

Skin and Sand

MEMORY OF A FORMER LOVE

Twenty-three years have gone by
Since that day in the river...

Cold water
Rising sky
And sand that squished between our toes
As noses touched naked in the sun...
In the evening
There was a chill in the touch of your hand
And on your skin
Was the taste of river sand.

I do not remember when we parted
Or even how we met,
Nor do I know if I loved you,
And yet,
As I muse beyond these middle years
I unearth an image of you ...
A face on a dry adobe wall ...
An unrestored mosaic ...
All that's left of you and me,
And the vision of tomorrows
That were never meant to be.

Loaded Guns

There are things to avoid
If life and love are going to last,
Loaded guns,
High places,
And lovers from your past.

Cocoa Butter

TEMPTATION AT THE BEACH

Her palm presses pink flesh,
Slides oil along a tender thigh,
And vows dissolve as I behold her,
Toe to head ...
Toasting in the sun ...
Butter melting into hot baked bread.

Cocoon

It was a dream I had dreamed before.
  I was little
  And the grass was tall
  And there was wind and sky
  And a red kite
  Whose string pulled against small hands
  As though the universe were a wish to fly
  And my string alone held earth in orbit.
I am awake now.
It is three a.m.
The woman I love is no longer here
And the stranger she has become lies beside me.

I have never before noticed my breath:
Air flows into my lungs …
Then out …
Then in again …
All on its own
As though someone knew
That if left alone
Men might close their eyes
And neglect to breathe again.

It is three-O-three a.m.
There is nothing inside me,
Only breath ...
Long deep breath that comes and goes on it own ...
And the smell of grass on a spring day
That floats in darkness
And will not go away.

Walk of Stone

THE SEPARATION

She told me of an earlier life
And showed me a picture of the little girl,
Then she played the music of our youth
And made grilled-cheese sandwiches.
There was red wine
And painted silk
And green crystal in the hollow of the moon,
And there were tears.
I left her when the rain stopped ...
Away the long walk of stones to an iron gate
And looking back,
A white dress in the hound-blue night,
And a rush of silence
Before the next footfall ... away,
Away ... the walk of stones.

Shattered Porcelain

I squeezed glue on each broken edge
And pressed it into place
While you held it at the base
And piece by piece
Our green porcelain parrot became one again.
There were tiny cracks and little spaces
From slivers lost somewhere on the floor
But it was late
And we can do no more.
Lovers do what lovers can …
Tomorrow we will try again.

Steel Cables

It blossomed fragile as a morning glory
The love of our youth,
How I loved you then!
We rolled in love like bear cubs.
Bold as the sun
I took you in my arms
And charged into our life.

And now the years have come and gone
Each taking its own shape
Like wild honeycomb,
Thick with the nectar of a thousand joys
And a thousand tears,
And sometimes . . .
It's hard to remember how I loved you then.
And sometimes it's hard to say how I love you now …

> *Like the steel cables*
> *They build bridges with*
> *That twist and swing through storms*
> *I love you.*

> *Like the force*
> *That makes our tree*
> *Sprout green buds each spring*
> *I love you.*

> *Like breath in my lungs*
> *And blood in my veins*
> *And tears in my eyes*
> *I love you.*

And I want little more
From this second half of life
Than to be with you,
And to love you tomorrow
As I have loved you today.

Romance?

A POET'S REVENGE

How do I love you?
I love the smell of your breath in the morning,
The tiny purple veins in your legs,
The you in the bathroom.
I guess I really do love you.

Breakfast
ON OUR TWENTIETH WEDDING ANNIVERSARY

This morning I brought you breakfast in bed:
    A sprig of mint,
    Hot buttered bread,
    And coffee.
Mint for hope,
Bread because you like it,
And coffee, without caffeine, for your ulcer.
Morning number seven thousand three hundred and five.
Our bed is warm,
Our children are healthy,
And we are alive.

Between the Sheets

I did not breathe hot kisses
On your neck tonight,
I did not leap unbridled
Into the pasture of your fantasies,
Nor did I hold your trembling nakedness
Against the body of my desire
For when I touched your hand
You drew it back
And curled into a ball,
Which I know from experience
Is a posture you intend to keep,
But it matters little after all
For somehow after all these years
Souls learned to love
While bodies sleep.

Aunt Mildred's Mistletoe

TO EILEEN SCHOEN

Through the plate glass window of her living room
She watched
As I stood with ropes and chains and teenage children
In the drizzling rain
Determined to harvest mistletoe
From the oak tree in her front yard.
Later at the Christmas party
She would tell the story ...
  How I threw the rope,
  And how each time it fell short
  And landed on the cars
  And how the kids just shook their heads
  And tried not to laugh at their Daddy,
  And how we danced in the rain
  When an entire branch came down
  With more mistletoe than we could carry.

She told the story again and again
And laughed each time
Till there were tears in her eyes,
And then she hugged me
As though I had performed some service for a queen.

I did not know how sick she was.
I did not know that soon
I would stand by her bed
As she closed her eyes —
Next year when we gather again
To light candles and sing songs
I will remember how you laughed
And how you hugged me.
I will remember the tree
Where the mistletoe once grew
And I will tell the children
So that they will remember too,
So in years to come,
When they stand beneath mistletoe
They will think of the tree
And the rain
And joy
And courage
And you.

On Mother's Day

TO MOM

You held me when I cried
And sang softly
Till I slept.

When I was hot with fever
You cooled my face
With a damp cloth
And fed me chicken soup.

After Saturday baseball games
When I stormed the kitchen
In victory or defeat
You prepared a feast.

With the smell of scotch pine,
Toys that danced,
Colored ribbons
And the nesting instinct of a robin red breast
You wove the warmth of Christmas into our home.

As constant as the rise and fall of the tide
With the fury of the sea
You birthed me
Nourished me
Taught me
Suffered and rejoiced with me
And helped me leave you to take a wife,
And by the life and joy of your grandchildren
I thank you for it all . . .
And I love you.

Orion

TO DAD

On a night with no moon
You turned my face to the sky,
Pointed your finger at three stars in a line,
Chanted the words of an ancient spell,
And conjured the hunter
To track the winter sky . . .
Where I see him still,
I see him with your eyes,
The sea-salt pearls of a father's eyes.

Resurrection

This evening
On the porch
Under my rocking chair,
I felt the crunch
Of a tiny, red, apparently indestructible dump truck.
On the steps
They had scattered a deck of Old Maid cards.
And as gold sun filled the branches of our tree
I heard the song of grandchildren...

> *Ring around the rosy,*
> *Pocket full of posies,*
> *Ashes,*
> *Ashes,*
> *We all fall down.*

Then I sensed you at the window behind me,
I felt your heart muscle throb in my chest
And as I turned to look into your eyes
I knew that this evening we would forego the sunset,
That instead we would make it rise.
Ashes ... ashes ...
We all fall down...
But till then, my love,
My forever-only love,
We will surely make it rise.

A Goodnight Poem

She lies beside me,
This sleepy goddess of my adolescent dreams.
"Can I write a poem for you?"
I ask.
She smiles and answers,
"Yes, if it's a short one."
And so it is:

Goodnight, my love.
May your dreams be sweet
As the life you have given me.

But as I finish
I see that I am too late
For she is already asleep.
I move closer
And whisper in her ear:

Goodnight, my love.
May your dreams be sweet
As the life you have given me.

And I know that some part of her has heard me
For she smiles,
And I feel it again . . .

Dreams — sweet as the life you have given me.
Goodnight, my love.

The Last Ride to St. Ben's

TO LOST FRIENDS

Our cars moved slowly through fog
On the long bridge over the lake,
Asphalt wound its path through pine wood,
The little bridge over the river
Rattled beneath our wheels
As it had a thousand times before,
And the breath of St. Ben's received us
Like childhood memory.
We will remember how it was today —
The stone chapel
The arched walkway
The grass
The mound of yellow clay
The pair of heavy boxes we leave behind . . .
And the wind,
The never-again forever wind.

Maybe A Red One

Don't let anyone dress me but my wife
When I'm blank eyes starting
From the other side of life,
And don't make me wear a tie
The morning after the day I die.

They'll say those things about me
As I breathe
The time will come
They'll calculate the sum of what I've done,
They'll talk about how this and that
The things I wrote
How I got fat
They'll talk me all the way into the ground
And then they'll go away.

But she will stay,
This woman I grow old with,
She will gather inside her
Those very last memories of me
And there is where I'll be.

So if I ever leave this life
Don't let anyone dress me but my wife,
And don't make me wear a tie
The day I die,
Except . . . maybe a nice red one.

About the Author

Brod Bagert is a husband, the father of four children, a former trial-lawyer, a former New Orleans City Councilman, and a poet who writes for child and adult audiences.

He has a passion for performing poetry, especially for children, and has become a popular speaker in schools and at teacher conferences. He believes that "the words of a poem on a printed page are like the notes of a song on sheet-music. Poetry comes alive when read out loud with feeling."

Acknowledgments

Thanks to Gary Esolen, who taught
me most of what I know about poetry
and how to write it. I also thank
Barbara Harding, whose editorial ear
has proved invaluable.

Other Books by Brod Bagert

For Adults

Alaska - Twenty Poems and a Journal $10.00

A Bullfrog at Café Du Monde $10.00
Poems from the Heart, Soul & Funny Bone of New Orleans

For Children

Let Me Be The Boss $15.00
Poems for Kids to Perform

Chicken Socks $16.00
And Other Contagious Poems

Elephant Games $16.00
And Other Playful Poems

Edgar Allen Poe $14.95
Poetry for Young Readers

Order by Mail
Juliahouse Fulfillment
6011 Chamberlain Dr.
New Orleans, LA 70122

(Include $2.00 per book for shipping & handling.)